D0537345

JUPITER
The Biggest Planet

by Chaya Glaser

Consultant: Karly M. Pitman, PhD
Planetary Science Institute
Tucson, Arizona

BEARPORT
PUBLISHING

New York, New York

Credits
Cover, © NASA; 4–5, © NASA/JPL/University of Arizona; 6–7, © Wikipedia & Nasa; 8,
© NASA; 9, © NASA/JPL/Space Science Institute; 10–11, © NASA/JPL/USGS; 12, © NASA/
JPL/USGS; 13, © NASA; 14, © NASA/JPL; 15, © Guido Amrein, Switzerland/Shutterstock;
16–17, © NASA/JPL; 18–19, © NASA/JPL/DLR; 21, © NASA/JPL/DLR; 23TL, © istock/
Thinkstock; 23TR, © NASA; 23BL, © NASA; 23BR, © Wikipedia/NASA.

Publisher: Kenn Goin
Senior Editor: Joyce Tavolacci
Creative Director: Spencer Brinker
Design: Deborah Kaiser
Photo Researcher: Michael Win

Library of Congress Cataloging-in-Publication Data

Glaser, Chaya, author.
  Jupiter : the biggest planet / by Chaya Glaser.
     pages cm. — (Out of this world)
  Includes bibliographical references and index.
  ISBN 978-1-62724-565-4 (library binding) — ISBN 1-62724-565-0 (library binding)
  1. Jupiter (Planet)—Juvenile literature. I. Title.
  QB661.G53 2015
  523.45—dc23
                                    2014037329

For more information, write to Bearport Publishing Company, Inc., 45 West 21st Street, Suite 3B,
New York, New York 10010. Printed in the United States of America.

10 9 8 7 6 5 4 3 2 1

CONTENTS

What's the biggest planet in our Solar System?

JUPiTER!

Jupiter is the fifth planet from the Sun.

JUPITER

MARS

VENUS

EARTH

MERCURY

SUN

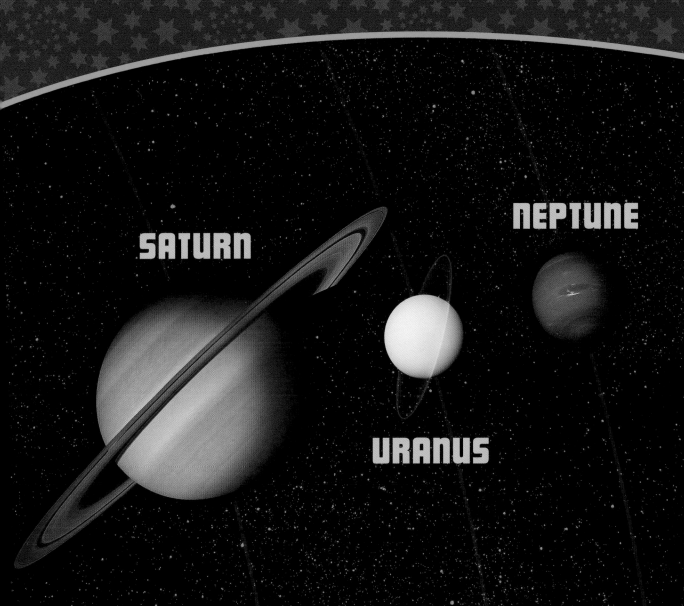

SATURN

URANUS

NEPTUNE

The planet is huge.

EARTH

More than 1,000 Earths could fit inside Jupiter.

JUPiTER

9

Jupiter is a giant ball of mostly **gases** and liquids.

It's covered with stripes.

The stripes are thick, gassy clouds.

Red, brown, yellow, and white stripes

There's a big spot on Jupiter.

The spot is a giant storm.

Storm

Close-up of storm on Jupiter

The storm started more than 300 years ago.

Winds on Jupiter can blow more than 425 miles per hour (684 kph).

A hurricane on Earth

That's twice as fast as Earth's strongest hurricane.

A **spacecraft**, Galileo, has circled Jupiter.

Its trip from Earth to Jupiter took six years.

Galileo

The spacecraft took photos
of Jupiter's 67 moons.

JUPiTER

These moons orbit, or travel around, the planet.

One of Jupiter's largest moons is Europa.

Scientists believe Europa has water.

Water means there could be life there!

JUPITER

EUROPA

JUPITER VERSUS EARTH

JUPITER	POSITION	EARTH
Fifth planet from the Sun	POSITION	Third planet from the Sun
86,881 miles (139,822 km) across	SIZE	7,918 miles (12,743 km) across
About –234°F (–148°C)	AVERAGE TEMPERATURE	59°F (15°C)
At least 67	NUMBER OF MOONS	One

GLOSSARY

gases (GASS-iz) substances that float in the air and are neither liquids nor solids; many gases are invisible

orbit (OR-bit) to travel around a planet, the Sun, or another object

Solar System (SOH-lur SISS-tuhm) the Sun and everything that circles around it, including the eight planets

spacecraft (SPAYSS-kraft) a vehicle that can travel in space

INDEX

READ MORE

Lawrence, Ellen. *Jupiter: The Giant of the Solar System (Zoom Into Space).* New York: Ruby Tuesday Books (2014).

Taylor-Butler, Christine. *Jupiter (Scholastic News Nonfiction Readers).* New York: Children's Press (2005).

LEARN MORE ONLINE

To learn more about Jupiter, visit
www.bearportpublishing.com/OutOfThisWorld

ABOUT THE AUTHOR

Chaya Glaser enjoys looking up at the stars and reading stories about the constellations. When she's not admiring the night sky, she can be found playing musical instruments.